Mud Matters

Mudstones and shales of Tarantula and Swap mesas stand below the Henry Mountain Wilderness, Capitol Reef National Park, Utah.

Mud
Matters

written and illustrated by
Jennifer Owings Dewey

photographs by
Stephen Trimble

MARSHALL CAVENDISH New York

In memory of Edward Abbey

ACKNOWLEDGMENTS

I'd like to thank my editor, Susan Albury, for accepting without hesitation the idea of a "personal" book on mud, a subject dear to my heart.

I would like to thank Stephen Trimble for his photographs and his contribution to the section on Sacred Clay, and Suzanne Page for her images of mudslinging and for reading the manuscript and giving me her wise and thoughtful comments.

Text and illustrations copyright © 1998 by Jennifer Owings Dewey
Photographs copyright © 1998 by Stephen Trimble,
except page 84, copyright © 1998 by Suzanne Page.
All rights reserved

Marshall Cavendish, 99 White Plains Road, Tarrytown, New York 10591

Library of Congress Cataloging-in-Publication Data
Dewey, Jennifer.
Mud matters / written and illustrated by Jennifer Owings Dewey.
p.   cm. Includes index. Summary: A personal account describing various uses of mud in such activities as ritual dancing, making pottery, building villages, constructing nests, playing games, and celebrating customs.
ISBN 0-7614-5014-9
1. Mud—Juvenile literature. [1. Mud.] I. Title.
QE471.2.D484   1998   553.6'1—dc21   97-32829   CIP   AC

The text of this book is set in 12 point Garamond Light.
The illustrations are rendered in pencil.
Printed in the United States of America
First edition
6 5 4 3 2

Contents

Mud curling in a desert wash, Cathedral Gorge State Park, Nevada

Introduction

I was a dry land kid, a desert rat growing up watching the skies for storms. Cloudbursts, flash floods, and quicksand were pure joy to me. Like a city kid who keeps secret the location of the best vacant lots for playing ball with her pals, I protected my favorite mud holes from invasion by strangers. From the earliest age, I had a lunatic love for the wettest, most thunderous rains. Bolts of lightning flashing in a stormy sky charged me with bursts of wild physical energy.

We lived in a part of the country where the rainy seasons are divided in two. The first is in April. These rains are mixed with blowing dust, hardly wetting the earth at all. More serious rains come in August and September, downpours, gully washers, and sometimes soft, gentle mists. These mists are so rare, only the oldest people we knew had ever experienced them.

In dry years when the storms never came, a hot wind blew, casting up clouds of parched earth in powdery drifts that rolled over the dirt roads and the flatlands like ghosts on the move. It was a fine white dust, the kind that gives you a sneezing fit even if you're not allergic.

In wet years the thunderstorms grew out of the eastern mountains like giant mushrooms, fungus shapes with swirling oval tops and thick gray stems formed by sheets and waves of falling rain.

Watching and waiting for rain was an occupation, like collecting fresh eggs from the henhouse or mowing the hay in the pasture.

If an adult found me staring at the sky and asked, "Why aren't you doing something useful?" I'd say, "I am. I'm watching for rain." It surprised me to be misunderstood.

Our place was a small ranch and pig farm in a valley between high mountain ranges. When a storm approached, the wind got to us long before the moisture did. It caught loose topsoil and blew it in streamers like reaching arms. Storm winds whipping in the tops of the trees made leafy branches reel and spin. The wind was confused, going every direction at once.

When the rain pounded down I danced barefoot in the thick of it, gleeful to be a part of the transformation of dust to loose, sticky mud. When the rain quit, I'd be half drowned and too wet to wring out.

The storms never lasted long, an hour, maybe two. The sky started out bright and clear, then turned blue black, and finally a livid, feverish yellow. The yellow tinge was caused by the filtering of the sun's rays through filmy sheets of rain.

Everything alive, the leaves on the trees, the wild grasses, the earth itself, smelled so sweet it made me dizzy.

In the fresh wetness of a passing storm, with afterwinds rushing madly, I chased the last of the shimmering raindrops to the riverbed, one of my favorite places to play.

1. Mud Between Your Toes

Flash Floods

Not a lot happened when I was a kid. The days and weeks that passed were what people call "uneventful." A crash on the two-lane paved road was cause for dropping everything and going to see the wreckage (and with luck, no dead bodies). A flash flood was an even bigger reason to quit whatever task was at hand and rush off to watch the water arrive.

The riverbed was a sun-bleached watercourse near our place, a bleak expanse of dry sand, except when it rained. I sat by the riverbed waiting for the flash flood I was certain was coming.

I smelled the flood first, and then heard the rushing roar of it. A fear of death by drowning, of being swept away never to be seen again, kept me a safe distance from the very edges where the flood-waters flowed.

Flash floods exploded out of the foothills in foaming heaves of muddy water, with crests three to five feet high and lesser heights flowing behind. Drowned pigs bobbed on the surface of the water, bellies to the sky, grabbed by the flood out of pens upstream. Mailboxes cruised past, silvery-slick in the light, sometimes still attached to their bases.

The floods took out bridges. The swell and press of water on ditch banks made the channels break down. Arroyos changed shape. Ripped-out tumbleweeds clogged the culverts. The water was a power, a force, especially in our landscape of dust, sand, and shallow-rooted trees and bushes.

Glorious Mud

After the flood went by and the waters subsided, we had mud, glorious mud.

If thunderstorms were blessings from the Water Gods, then mud was a gift from the Children of these mysterious Spirits. That is what I believed back then.

Mud squished deliciously between my toes and rippled against my legs. It slipped through my fingers like liquid gold and washed up over the tops of the ditches and the irrigation ponds. I'd plunge into it, trying to sink out of sight. Mud was alive and squirming with half-suffocated insects, beetles with all their legs kicking in frantic efforts to be free. It was smelly with rot or aromatic, like a heady perfume my mother might use. It smelled like death or something just born.

Mud sparkled and shone if it contained mica, a mineral washed out of the nearby mountains. It was sometimes decorated with surface patterns of flowers or frost. In winter, when it was frozen and lacy with ice, it looked good enough to eat.

There was slick, smooth mud, like satin, and pebbled mud with grit in it. Some was cracked and scarred with lines like earthquake zones. We had the oily kind, and mud that was grainy and chunky.

From my first memory of paying attention to mud, I loved all kinds, every one.

Drying pothole, Ute Canyon, Colorado National Monument, Colorado.

Sinkholes and Quicksand

After the rains came and went, and the sun was once more a yellow fire in a cloudless blue sky, I'd go looking for quicksand.

Quicksand is mysterious mud. Something sinister lurks in its murky depths. Quicksand is old mud. It takes years for quicksand to be seasoned, to simmer, cook, and ripen until it's done.

A drought comes, a rainless year, and quicksand dries up. You might think it's dead, parched beyond recovery. It isn't. As soon as it rains, no matter how long that takes, the quicksand hole awakens, good as new. There are quicksand holes legendary and enduring enough to be marked on old-time maps, the way poison-free water holes are shown.

Quicksand holes go along getting better and better like pots of soup on the back of the stove, never fussed with much but not forgotten.

The surface of a quicksand hole is greasy-looking, with bubbles rising, floating, then popping soundlessly. The bubbles shine and glisten in the sun, like tiny gemstones. Below the surface the mud is layered, the way homemade mayonnaise gets when it stands too long. The ingredients are separated out.

Below the part you can see and reach into, it's impossible to know what goes on. Do quicksand holes have bottoms? and if they do, are they hard or soft? hot or cold?

Quicksand differs from one landscape to another. In Arabia quicksand needs no water to be destructive. A broad plain of smooth sand may conceal a trench hundreds of feet deep. Those who cross such a plain can be devoured in sliding rivers of sand from which there is no escape.

To me, the world's very best quicksand was found where I grew up, simply because I knew no other. I'd sit at the edge of a quick-sand hole and listen to the gurgling and hissing of the mud, signs that would tell me the hole was old, ripe, and dangerous. I'd test the sucking qualities by tossing in sticks or rocks and counting the seconds these objects took to disappear below the surface. That is one way to measure the potency and power of a quicksand hole.

Another way is to get into it. With all the lingering I did around quicksand, it wasn't until the summer I turned eleven that I got my own firsthand experience with the power of this strange mud.

Knowing it was dangerous, aware I'd be scolded for sure if I was seen taking such a risk, I decided to step into a quicksand hole anyhow. I had the childish notion that I'd come out alive, no matter what. (I took a stout willow stick with me, just in case, though.)

I picked a hole and settled into it with my heart in my throat. I looked down and watched the knobs of my kneecaps slip from sight below the bubbling surface. The mud took me willingly, its coolness a gentle coaxing, not sudden or violent. It drew me inch by slow inch. Spellbound, excited and terrified, I listened to the eerie mur-mur and guzzle of sucking noises, a soft whoosh in my ears.

I tried to be calm. That ended quickly. In less than five minutes I was ready to get out, to be released from the slippery, shivery muck urging me down. I rotated my body one full turn, my arms raised and the willow stick waving. I pictured myself going out of sight, as pioneer wagons once had, lost in quicksand beds, women and children, and oxen, too, vanishing in the bubbling depths of the sucking mud.

The willow stick, sturdy as it was, saved me.

It took a lot of effort, heaving and leaning landward, yanking with all my strength to raise one foot, then the other. The quicksand was fierce in the end. Even with hard thrusts and sharp hip-swivels,

I might still be there but for the stick, which I used as a lever once I had it planted firmly in the solid bank of the hole.

Once out, I sat gasping, hot in the sun, my legs and most of my upper body coated with thick, shiny mud. I felt like an oiled pig at a county fair. I watched the surface reorganize itself and counted my blessings for being on steady ground. Soon the quicksand was as greasy as before, quiet but for the surge of rising bubbles.

My experiment was over. I was satisfied that quicksand has a well-deserved reputation for being dangerous.

The World's First Ooze

One day an adult in our neighborhood was out in the hills, exploring, when he came upon a fossilized bone. He told people it was millions of years old. His discovery was the talk of the valley for a while, about the oldness of the bone, that it was part of an animal no longer in existence on Earth, and how it came to be preserved as a fossil.

I remember asking a lot of questions around me about the mysterious bone. My mother got my mind racing when she said, "If you find primordial ooze maybe you'll get lucky and find fossils of your own."

"Primordial ooze? What's that?" I pestered.

After I grilled my mother to tell all she knew, she finally said, in exasperation, "All I know is, life supposedly began in primordial ooze. It's some kind of mud, and probably a lot like the mud you're so fond of playing in!"

I went looking for primordial ooze in the most logical place I could think of, down by the river, the real river.

The Rio Grande, west of where I lived, ran out of the north

Mud along the Escalante River, Glen Canyon National Recreation Area, Utah.

with a steady flow of greenish brown water. The river was not always high, but it never dried up. There was mud along its banks, reliable mud, meaning it stayed wet, soggy, and squashy all year round, even in the hottest weeks of summer.

Before exploring for the primordial ooze my mother vaguely knew about, I read as much as I could about life's origins, in books and encyclopedias we had on our shelves. Our supply of books in those days was pathetically small, but I was able to discover a few crucial facts.

Life did (as my mother suspected) begin with a chemical "soup" of ingredients that cooked for billions of years, changing in content as the earth itself changed. Rain fell in torrents from turbulent skies, pooling in depressions in rocks and deep cracks in the earth's surface. Seas washed over the young earth, retreating and then flowing across the land again. Heat and warmth from the sun heated and "cooked" the brew. Finally conditions were exactly right for bacteria to form, assemble, and thrive.

I believed primordial ooze must still exist. If it happened on Earth once, why not again? I saw nothing to stop me from finding it. If anything, it would be better ooze than before because of being older.

I crawled on the mud by the Rio Grande, mud of different colors and textures. As I crawled I imagined what the planet was like billions of years earlier, before the first cells came together to give birth to bacteria. I thought I could hear ancient sea waves crash against shores where no creatures stirred. Winds blew in birdless skies. The breezes did not rustle leaves on trees because there were no trees.

My vision of the prehistoric past gave me the energy and determination to crawl more vigorously. I followed my nose as much as I searched with my eyes. I reasoned that primordial ooze would have a stench to it. Most old mud smells bad, with all the comings and goings of animals living and dead.

When I discovered shallow basins of stagnant water at the river's edge, my hopes soared. Gobs and clumps of slime floated on quiet water surfaces, which glistened with translucent film. Everything was still but for an occasional water bug slipping sideways in the murk.

The slime had movement to it. It breathed. Along with the surface shine, quivering bubbles in fine layers were attached to the slime, like droplets of dew clinging to spider webs after rain.

I stuck my fingers in, slowly and with the hesitation that comes when you fear a single touch will ruin something perfect. The slime twitched when I caressed it with my fingertips. It reminded me of touching my cat when she was asleep. A tiny section of furry skin would shiver under my hand, but no other part of the cat would move.

When I blew on the slime it seemed to shrink, like a blade of grass bending away from the wind. The water under the slime appeared to be gluey-thick with a jellylike texture. The closer I looked the more I saw teeny animals swimming in the shadowy depths.

The slime had all the requirements of primordial ooze, according to my vision of it. It smelled awful. The sun beat down and cast rays of light across the slime and the underlying water. The colors went from greenish blue to bluish brown. Around my head the atmosphere was warm and hushed, matching the sense I had of this discovery being just what I'd been looking for: ancient, ageless primordial ooze.

I closed my eyes to better imagine myself as a bacteria, a

startling new organism floating in that gently swaying ooze, warm and with everything just right.

It wasn't easy to picture myself a one, two, or three-celled animal, or the earth as it must have been as a freshly formed planet billions of years ago.

Thinking about how much Earth-time had passed since life began, more years than I could fathom, I decided the ooze where bacteria first appeared must have dried up and disappeared long before I was born, or any other human, or the dinosaurs for that matter.

So many billions of years had passed, I could not expect to find the earliest ooze. The slime I sniffed out was just slime, nothing more.

Searching for Fossils

A flock of ravens landed on the river mud and I found myself watching them, distracted from musing over ooze. They bounced and flapped their dark wings with high energy, eager to drill into the mud with their beaks, to poke with their toes and find tiny animals to gobble up.

I watched the flock and decided to pretend to be a raven rather than a bacterium. It made more sense to imagine myself a larger animal than one you could hardly see with your eyes, and it would be more fun.

The ravens showed me what digging could do.

I started to poke and scrape at the mud, ready to find treasure: naked mole rats in colonies, eyeless under the mud, the chambers of their vast cities stashed with food and with babies no bigger than thimbles.

Ravens

Instead I found bones.

The first piece or chunk I uncovered was reddish white and heavy, with the weight of stone, not bone. It had a dark marrow in it. I scraped at the marrow with my fingernail. It was like iron, purplish black and solid.

I held my discovery in both hands and spat on it, then rubbed it hard with the heel of my hand. The bone was revealed, white with lots of darkish lines running through it. It was dappled with pores that looked like pockmarks on skin.

I jumped up and turned in a circle, my heart thumping in my chest. What a find! Somehow I knew it was important. It must be as old as the hills, probably much older. I would find out. I would ask the neighbor with the fossilized bone.

The man was happy to tell me what he thought about my find. It turned out he was an expert on the subject. He said my treasure was about twenty million years old, part of the thigh section of an animal called a Camalops, a camellike creature with a long neck, no hump, and hooves like a horse.

Camalops

"It's really no wonder we find these fossilized bones," the man told me. "After all, what are now arid, thirsty, cactus-covered flats were once lush, waving grasslands where ancient animals moved in huge herds across this valley. Camalops, and other grazers of the distant past, lived the way sheep and cows do today. Antelopes existed then, and rhinoceroses, prehistoric pigs, dogs, and horses."

After hearing all this, I went back to the river and dug like a crazy person, determined to find the rest of the Camalops.

The neighbor had described the kind of ground most likely to yield fossilized bones, and he was right. I searched on greenish soil near the river, up slope from the muddy banks, and found more bone chips than I could keep track of. They'd been there all the time, but I hadn't been looking for them.

Below the surface of the green soil, and in the soft, thick mud at water's edge, I dug out bones riddled with holes like air pockets in volcanic rock. In this spot the real "grave" of Camalops was centered. The bulk of this animal's remains had lain undisturbed and still for twenty million years.

My expert neighbor told me that the fossilized Camalops bones were the remains of hard body parts, not soft ones. When an animal dies of old age, or from death in the jaws of a predator, what falls to the ground is eaten by parasitic insects, or parched by the sun and blown away as dust.

The bones sometimes last awhile, and some of the teeth, and maybe a portion of the rotting hide. When an animal dies in mud and lies there, coated and sealed, its remains vanish from sight. Mud protects as well as seals. It slips and slides over the dead animal and blankets the body in a coating insects cannot get through and the sun cannot bleach.

Many fossil remains are not the hard, bony parts of animals at all, just impressions in mud once soft, now hardened, of what were living creatures millions of years ago. Delicate winged insects such as dragonflies landed in mud and got stuck. The flesh gone, what we see are imprints of their fine bodies, ghostly traces of what they were.

Fossils of all kinds, however they come to be, may stay hidden in the ground. Unless they are washed out, eroded by water, or lifted and exposed by movement within the earth, they are never seen by human eyes. With my own discovery I suspected many more Camalops must be concealed in the hills and valleys up and down the river and in the surrounding country.

Twenty million years before, in the desert that I knew, rain had fallen often and animals had had plenty to eat and drink.

No wonder Camalops liked it here.

It wasn't possible to know what killed the Camalops I found. I thought these leftovers had worked their way to the surface so that I, or someone like me, might find them. It crossed my mind that I'd be a fossil one day. When the time came that I was bent and withered with age, I'd find a muddy hole to lie down in and die.

Maybe I'd be the discovery of someone living in a time too distant in the future to imagine.

Plaidont Skull, from around 136 years ago.

2. Ritual Mud

Mudheads

"Look out." Rose, a friend my age, hissed a warning into my ear. "The Mudheads are coming."

I saw them, ten dancers descending a ladder from a rooftop, coming to earth and landing with exaggerated movements, their arms over their heads. The dancers wiggled their hips as if they were doing some childish dance.

The Mudheads wore nothing but tiny black kilts tied to their waists, so their private parts didn't show but you could plainly see their backsides. Their bodies were smeared with pink mud, every inch, so not even the smallest patch of regular skin showed through. They looked as if their bodies, heads and all, had been molded by a giant's hand out of sticky, pink clay.

The Mudheads pranced in a line, like a string of fat beads, weaving right and left, making motions to the crowd. Their arms punched at the air. They thrust their fingers up in rude gestures.

The people watching, like Rose and I, got quiet once the Mudheads were moving around in the dance plaza.

"If you're afraid don't let them see," Rose said in a whisper. "Or else they'll torment you especially."

I kept still and hardly dared breathe, my face as blank and free of expression as I could make it. I'd watched Mudheads before. I knew them as teasers, the clowns, the dancers who played mean and silly tricks. We were at Zuni Pueblo, and these Mudheads were the Zuni clowns. They danced around with more serious dancers and made a game of being both funny and scary.

The Mudheads circled the inner line of spectators. The crowd seemed to take in breath as if all were one creature, watching with a single pair of eyes instead of hundreds. Everyone waited to see what the Mudheads would do.

I heard a drum and knew the dance was beginning, a plea for rain, a ceremony held in the spring and summer months at Zuni. The Mudheads were coming close enough to give me goose bumps, even though the air temperature was near one hundred degrees. The drum was the throb of an insect's song in my ears.

I watched jouncing mud-painted bellies and belly buttons caked with pink clay and naked bodies smeared so you could pick out the tracks of fingers. Had the Mudheads covered themselves with pink clay? Or had someone sacred, a clan chief, a ceremony leader, done this for them?

A Mudhead dropped down in front of me, bobbing like an owl. The broad, mud-smeared back of the dancer glistened in the sun, shiny from a mixture of mud and body moisture.

The Mudhead grabbed my leg and pulled off my sneaker. Like a crazy thing, the dancer beat the earth with the shoe, as if furious with rage at how pathetic and worn it was. The pounding raised a small storm of dust. Then the Mudhead leaped up and ran, darting right and left like a character in a bad movie escaping the police.

For seconds I didn't move, not even to blink an eye. A lizard-brain instinct warned me to stay still. The other Mudheads stole

Mudhead figure

shoes from people all around, men, women, children, even babies.
The group of Mudheads formed up and ran in loopy circles,
waving their shoe-prizes in the air, triumphant and ridiculous. They
made no sounds, as if they had no voices to speak with; they frisked

with their feet, exuberant and delighted at having tricked us out of our footwear.

"We'll get your sneaker back later," Rose said softly. For some reason they'd left her feet alone.

I didn't care if I ever saw my sneaker again. It made no difference one way or the other. I would give up my other sneaker, too, if any of the wild dancers wanted it. I wasn't about to put up a struggle for possession of my shoes against a Spirit from another world.

The afternoon at Zuni was filled with heat and visions. The figures of men and women in bright costumes, in bone and turtle shell rattles, feathers, and pelts from foxes and coyotes, beat a rhythm on the dance plaza surface.

Their feet were covered in beaded leather moccasins trimmed with porcupine quills and fur. The beat was a pulse connected, like a thread you couldn't see, to the throbbing of the drums. Dust came off the hundreds of moving feet, dust that choked our throats and noses. To clear breathing passages, people wrapped their mouths with bandannas.

The Mudheads acted crazy and silly all afternoon. They played tug-of-war, and chase, and keep-away. They held a pretend marriage ceremony, using a "stolen" girl and boy from the crowd as the bride and groom.

The Mudheads held my attention. I was afraid to let down my guard, sure I'd be grabbed myself if I showed the slightest indication of fear. I had seen Mudheads capture children, wrap them in ropes, and keep them that way for hours while the dance went on all around.

The clay-painted mud spirits kept watch over their pile of shoes as if it were gold. A single Mudhead was in charge, waving people (and dogs) away if they came too close. I could not imagine finding my own sneaker among all the other shoes heaped in the dust.

I watched, shading my eyes with my hands, and when the dancers slipped away I was sorry, even though I felt tired and stiff from such a long time looking. A sense of being a small part of something big and significant came with observing such a dance.

The Mudheads remained after the other dancers left. They stood quietly, obediently, like children waiting for permission to leave the playground.

An old man with a creased and wrinkled face came out of the house where the ladder was propped, the ladder the Mudheads had used to reach the ground when the day of dancing began. He wore a bright yellow shirt and freshly washed blue jeans. His gray hair was in long braids, and a bandanna was tied around his head, above the ears and over his brow. The Mudheads watched him approach and then they gathered around him in a circle, enclosing him.

The old man took a leather pouch from his pocket. He sprinkled meal from the little bag into the palm of a hand. "Sacred meal," Rose whispered. "The clan chief is the only person who can let the Mudheads go. Watch."

The old man doused all the Mudheads, one by one, with the sacred meal, making sure the yellow powder landed on their mud-covered shoulders and backs. Then the old man waved his arm, a gesture that said, "Go. Leave now." And the Mudheads did.

The Mudheads looked tired. Their shoulders were slumped and their heads were bowed. It was sad to see them, with their posture of dejection, climb the ladder and disappear.

I had hardly noticed, preoccupied with the Mudheads and the dance, but while the afternoon passed, thunderheads had billowed up over the eastern mountains.

When the Mudheads left, the sky was dark with approaching

thunder and rain. Lightning flashed in the distance. I took Rose by the sleeve of her shirt and pointed wordlessly to the pile of shoes. It was reduced to half its original size.

Together we ran to the pile and began tossing shoes this way and that. Other children did the same, looking for their own missing shoes. It started to rain, a cold, slashing wetness blowing sideways against us. By the time I found my sneaker, we were soaked and shivering.

We were mud-splashed to the knees when we reached a small wooden door that led inside the house where Rose's grandparents lived. Soon the two of us were drying off with cotton towels, huddled close to the wood stove, listening to the rain pound on the roof, loud and rushing, like sea waves dropped from the heavens.

Rose's grandfather said, "Get dry. Get into fresh clothes. We'll talk."

It was a night of storytelling, of learning about Mudheads while gnawing ears of roasted corn and dipping tortillas in hot bowls of green chili. (I had a million questions). And it was a night of steady rain. It was the kind of rain the old man called a "one-hundred-year rain," saying, "It only comes like this once in a hundred years."

The storm continued outside while the old man spoke in a soft, low voice. He said, "The Mudheads have a Zuni name. It is *Molanhaktu*. The first white people to see these dancers covered with clay called them 'Mud Heads,' and 'Muddyheads,' and we still use the nickname. It is easier to say 'Mudheads' than *'Molanhaktu.'*"

Rose's grandfather explained that Mudheads are smeared with pink clay because they are goblins, not fully human. They are supposed to scare children, to tease.

"Mudheads talk to the Spirits, the Great Water Serpent especially. They are messengers between humans and Spirits and use their powers to urge the Spirits to bring rain. The Mudheads do us a great service. They battle with the Great Water Serpent on behalf of the Zuni people so the crops will not fail for lack of moisture."

"Where are the Mudheads from?" I asked, remembering their mysterious descent on a ladder from a rooftop.

"They come from the clouds," Rose's grandfather answered. "They are Sacred Beings, and they live in the Underworld when they are not with us, helping with our ceremonies."

The explanation left me puzzled. I understood the Mudheads as clowns. I had seen with my own eyes their crazy actions and teasing ways. It was where they came from, where they lived, and how they moved from place to place that mystified me.

Mudheads, I thought, are creatures only half human, and yet they are able to discuss important matters like the coming of rain with Spirits dwelling where no human dares venture.

I dreamed about Mudheads that night. I saw them standing on their heads in the dirt, rolling in mud and rubbing their naked bodies. In my dreams they whirled and leaped and bounced between the earth and the sky, until they vanished into the clouds like smoke.

When Clay Is Sacred

When I first met Jason he was five years old, the youngest member of a Pueblo family I knew because the eldest girl, Michelle, was my friend and classmate. Jason liked to sit next to his mother's basin of red, sticky clay and dig into it with his hands. The rest of us children liked to do the same, but only Jason ever made objects worth keeping. He shaped small, recognizable figures of dogs, sheep, goats, and horses.

Jason's mother was plainly proud of the boy's sculptures. "He likes the feel of the mud against his skin, yes?" she would say. She'd smile at her little son, who wore an expression of complete concentration when working with the clay. "Nobody taught him to handle the clay," Jason's mother continued. "When I first saw him doing this I thought to myself, he likes the sparkle, the glitter."

The clay sparkled and shimmered because crushed mica, a silvery mineral, had been added to it.

I would watch the boy and, in spite of his serious face, see his pleasure, the obvious satisfaction he got from squashing the clay between his fingers, rubbing and twisting it into the shapes he wanted.

Jason's mother and maternal grandmother are both artists with clay, the mud that flows from the earth and is used to make jars, plates, bowls, and figures such as Jason's. It is a long tradition in Jason's family, female relatives who work with the clay. The women talk about the clay in hushed, respectful voices, calling it sacred because it is a gift from Mother Earth.

Pueblo artists use no machines in their work. They have strong opinions about the tools they use. Whereas Jason was content to manipulate the clay with his fingers, adult artists use natural objects, small, smooth stones from the river for polishing, or strips of gourd dried in the sun until they feel like leather. They paint designs on pots, bowls, or plates using brushes made with the shredded fibers of the yucca plant.

Yucca brushes last longer, and apply the paint better, than store-bought brushes. Clay is coiled, rolled, smeared, slipped, slapped, caressed, and treated, in every way, as sacred.

The old ways work well, but artists stick to these methods for another reason. Familiar, proven habits are a way to deepen connections to the past, to ancestors, to those who came before.

Hopi potter Bessie Namoki shapes a pot from clay and paints it with a yucca brush, Hopi Pueblos, Arizona.

As a child I played with mud, building with it, coiling lengths of it into crude bowls, but it wasn't the same for me as for Jason. For my people mud is mud, clay is clay, and there is nothing special about it. People in my culture make more of sand castles on the beach than pots formed with clay taken from the ground.

The Pueblo people, and other Native Americans, cherish the clay because it creates a bond between themselves and the earth. Transforming mud from lumps of shapeless stickiness into shiny pots decorated with graceful designs is evidence and proof of something "born" of the earth and dependent on it for existence.

Jason goes with his female relatives to collect the clay from sites kept secret from outsiders. Before they remove the clay from the earth, the potters sprinkle sacred meal over the ground, a gesture to give thanks. The women say prayers for the presence of the clay. They express gratitude for being able to take clay away.

At home the clay is strained, soaked, and strained again. Impurities are taken out. Sometimes crushed mica or ashes are added.

"When it is time to make a pot, to roll the coils that will become the walls, I wait and listen and watch the clay, to learn what it wishes to become." Jason's mother speaks these words to describe how she makes a pot. "The clay talks to me," she says. "If I don't pay attention, if I just do what I want, the clay won't work for me."

Artists in clay tell how it feels when something breaks, when a much-labored-over pot cracks in the kiln during firing. "A part of me goes with it," a clay artist says. "I am diminished by the loss, and I have to begin again, to make another pot."

And begin again they do. The clay, and what is made with it, and the way these objects are fashioned—all of this is sacred.

Mudslinging

"Here is something hard to believe," a Hopi friend named Dan once told me. "Adult people throwing mud at each other for a reason. It's a Hopi custom we call Mudslinging."

"Tell me," I urged. I'd never heard of Mudslinging. It sounded like fun to have a reason to throw mud at somebody.

"Marriage is a solemn passage among the Hopi," Dan said. "In our villages the wedding ceremonies go on for a week. The day before the wedding, the groom's father visits the bride's house. He knocks on the door and insists on being let in. With him are other members of the groom's family: aunts and uncles, sisters and brothers.

"Those inside the house open the door just a crack and say, 'Who are you? What do you want?' They act like they don't know him. 'War is declared!' the groom's father announces loudly. He pushes the door open and then the craziness begins."

Dan pauses before going on with his story. He grins, his dark eyes shiny with humor.

"The groom and his family have secretly prepared buckets of mud, which they have brought with them. The mud is four different colors, one for each of the four directions: north, south, east, and west. It is sacred mud. These people rush into the bride's house and grab everyone, including the bride, and drag them out into the yard. The groom's family dig into the buckets of mud and begin throwing it, smearing it on every person they can catch. The bride's family dip into the mud, too. Before long the yard is swarming with people of all ages, from babies to old grandmothers and grandfathers, flinging mud at each other as if they've lost their minds."

"While this goes on, some of the mud throwers yell insults back

Mudslinging at the Hopi Pueblos, Arizona.

and forth at each other. It is the aunties of the groom who do this. They say how ugly the bride is, what a terrible cook her mother is, things like that."

I laughed to hear this. "What happens next?" I asked. Dan was eager to continue his description of the Mudslinging.

"If the bride's people are able to catch the groom's father, they hold him down and give him a haircut. This makes him feel foolish. It's an insult." Dan's grin widened. "The Mudslinging ends peacefully. Once the buckets are emptied and everyone is coated with mud, the participants shake hands and make peace. Food is shared, a feast of corn and mutton, a lot of food."

"And the wedding takes place the next day?" I asked.

"Yes," Dan said, a wistful expression appearing on his handsome face. "This is how it was for me when I got married. There was much hilarity, and sacred rituals, too, and then I became a husband, no longer a single man."

"Why do they do the Mudslinging? Was it fun when it happened to you? Or was it horrible?"

"It was a lot of fun. Maybe the reason for it is to get troubles over with in a happy way before the marriage, the mother-in-law problems, the father-in-law problems."

I nodded. It made sense.

"When two families come together and become joined, there are always disputes. It's expected. Mudslinging gets everyone's energy for arguing out of the way, at least for a while," Dan added. A thoughtful smile came to his face when he was finished with his storytelling.

3. Building Mud

Building Miniature Mud Villages

Floodwaters were approaching, creeping with a languid sluggishness toward the village. The water was silvery and flat, coming inch by inch, lapping at the soil like a thirsty tongue.

The mud village was quiet. Nothing stirred in the dirt streets. No living thing slipped in or out of a doorway. The town appeared resigned to its fate, to be devoured and consumed in the flood.

The village was built with mud, with bricks of hard-packed soil set one on top of another. There were a dozen small houses, with low walls around them for privacy. The architecture was traditional southwestern style, no building more than two stories high and most having only one.

The town square was also enclosed by a wall. At one corner stood the church. The structure had a pair of bell towers shaped like upside-down ice-cream cones rising above the front entrance.

In back of the church there was a meeting hall with many windows in its walls. The doors of the church and meeting hall were two features in the village made with wood, not mud.

A cemetery was marked out at the east side of the meeting hall. Stones had been carefully placed to indicate which grave was which.

A few trees had been planted around the headstones in the ceme-tery. With the exception of these trees, the mud village was bare of any landscaping.

Because the village was made of hard mud dried in the sun, it would take no time at all for the floodwaters to reduce it to ruins.

A single pair of eyes watched the impending disaster. This

Mud village

observer was a giant compared to the size of the village, as big as Gulliver was to the Lilliputians. She lay on the ground inches from the outer wall that surrounded the village.

She was a ten-year-old girl, and she'd constructed the village, from the first miniature brick to the last. She'd used her fingertips to carefully dab soft, loose mud on the walls of the buildings, smoothing it until it rippled like frosting on a cake. She took great pride in the village she had made.

She was also determined to see the village destroyed by the flood. From the moment the girl had started her village, she had known how it would all end. When the crops growing nearby were irrigated, water would spill, as it always did, over low banks of dirt surrounding the fields. The water would come slowly, easily, and without a sound.

Building miniature villages with painstaking care and then watching the irrigation water come and drown her work was a ritual the girl had loved since an early time in her life. The building was hypnotic and involving. In the midst of making a village the girl missed meals, forgetting she was hungry. The hours she spent making tiny bricks were impossible to count.

The destruction was thrilling and strange, both at once. After a village was washed away, she started on a new one. Rebuilding was part of the mysterious joy she gained from the whole process.

One summer the girl and her two older sisters worked on their own villages, each about six feet square. The villages were connected by roads. The three of them constructed bridges over miniature washes and drilled tunnels through banks of dirt. They used toy cars and trucks from the dime store in town to transport the imaginary population from one place to another.

The system of twisting, turning dirt roads became channels the water rushed down when the irrigation season started and the ditches overflowed. The girl and her sisters stood ankle deep in swishing, whispering surges of muddy water, watching their structures melt away to nothing.

I was the watching girl. The towns were mine. I placed my miniature villages at the low end of the biggest alfalfa field, positioning them so their fates were sealed even before I finished building.

Now and then we saved our villages. We drew plans for them, making sure they were out of the path of the irrigation water

When a flood did come, and total devastation was inevitable, we warned the imaginary population, giving them time to pack up and evacuate. Once the water subsided and reconstruction started, the pretend people were allowed to return.

I was once asked why I took such pains to build mud villages, only to see them swept away. The answer is shrouded in childhood imagining, in a world that existed inside my head back then. If the life I lead today allowed for spending a summer crawling around in the dirt on my hands and knees, laying miniature mud bricks, I'd do it in an instant, knowing rain or irrigation water would surely wipe out all my efforts.

Animal Builders

The wasp shone shiny black except for its orange abdomen. It landed lightly on the surface of the mud in the mud puddle, as if it didn't wish to ruin the perfection of its slender, glossy body in the brown muck.

The wasp reached forward with two thin front legs, a praying gesture. It worked quickly to take up a glob of mud and roll it into a neat ball. It flew away.

The wasp carried the mud ball under its chin, safely between its two front claws. Its wings were a blur in flight.

When I was still a kid I watched this scene with my body flat on the ground at the edge of the mud puddle. The wasp was back in minutes, this time with company. A dozen or more wasps just like it swarmed down to land on the mud and begin gathering it up, rolling tiny bits into balls the size of pinheads.

I counted flights to and from the mud and quickly lost track. The wasps showed no signs of weariness with their task of mud-getting. It was the opposite. They seemed to become increasingly dedicated to their work the longer they did it.

After a while I got tired of lying on my stomach. I went to see if I could find the site where the insects were building their colony.

I followed a dusky trail of wasps flying through the bright spring air and watched them land on the barn wall, up high, near the roof-line. The mud nests were taking shape, more than fifty of them, spaced inches apart.

I got a ladder and leaned it against the old barn planking. By climbing the ladder and reaching the height of the nests, I could easily see what the wasps were doing.

They stuffed their mud wads in their mouths and chewed until the saliva-mud mixture was the consistency they needed. Then, with actions so quick it was hard to see them, the wasps daubed the mud in place, creating rows and rows of fragments that formed the walls of their nests. Each wasp worked alone, as if oblivious of any other, and yet they placed their nests close together. The wasps must have gained protection from the large colony, the idea of there being safe-ty in numbers.

To finish their building the wasps used wet, slippery mud and spread it on the sides of their constructions, plastering the delicate-looking walls until they were smooth like brown silk. They used their legs, feet, and mouths as tools.

Each nest sloped gently toward the ground, with a slight bend in its shape. I realized with amazement that the wasps built their nests to shed rain, not only by placing them under the roof of the barn, but by designing them with a slant.

With the nests complete, the wasps began to lay their eggs. Each one stuck its back end into its own mud chamber and for long moments stayed perfectly still. When this was done they all began to collect spiders and other meaty morsels, which they rendered senseless with their potent venom.

The wasps packed the stunned, but not dead, prey into the nest chambers where the eggs were safely stashed. These became the food supply for the wasp larvae after they hatched. The larvae would have plenty of fresh meat to eat as they developed. When they were full-grown adult wasps, they would chew through the mud walls that confined them and fly away.

Wasp building a nest with mud

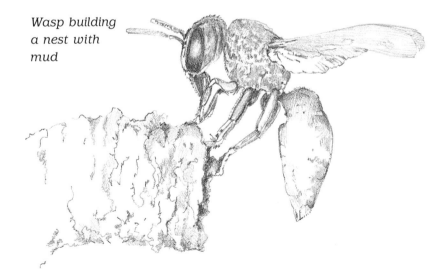

To me as a child it was an astonishing system, and it remains so. Female wasps do the work, building nests for their eggs, preparing for the next generation. Their investment of energy is enormous. It pays off with swarms of young wasps bursting out each spring.

The nest-building activities of mud-daubing wasps marked the end of winter. So did the arrival of barn and cliff swallows, birds that also use mud to build their nests.

Our place provided enough spring mud that even the most discriminating and picky animal builder would find what it needed. We had pig, cow, horse, and chicken mud. We had duck mud. There were smelly black pits of mud around the stock tanks. The mud in the lower pastures was thick and certain most times of year, but especially in the spring when the snow melted and the soggy ground made a mess of everything.

Every year when spring came around, our horse wrangler, Bill, swore he was ready to move to a mud-free acre of ground. He never left, so I guess there is no such place on Earth.

I watched the swallows when they came, to see which mud they'd choose. The barn swallows didn't like the mud that the cliff swallows favored. They added grass and straw to their mud before building with it, which the cliff swallows never did. The barn swallows often chose mud from the lower pasture, where the milk cows grazed; pigs got in under the fence, and so did chickens, who had the freedom to go where they wanted. It was smelly, thick mud laced with stems and roots, just right for barn swallow nests.

Both birds worked in a feverish hurry to get their nests built, as if the eggs were already sitting near the bottoms of the female birds, ready to slide out.

The males and females cooperated, each doing a share of the nest building.

Cliff Swallow nests under Interstate highway bridge, Clear Creek Canyon, Utah.

The birds were messy, not fastidious like the wasps. Soon after beginning their construction projects, their feathers were smeared with mud and hunks of it hung from their toes and beaks.

The swallows were quick. They zoomed past my head so fast, I heard the rush of wings and barely saw the birds themselves. Small, with graceful, pointed wings, the swallows showed how animal mud works to make a shelter, if you have a plan.

The swallows built up nest walls with bits of mud smashed together and tucked one against the other, like bricks. The birds used the sides of their beaks like trowels to smooth the final, outer layers of mud. They collected spider silk, dried grass, and feathers to line their nests when the work of building was finished.

The nests were ideal containers for fragile eggs, and sturdy enough to safely house the featherless nestlings while they grew up. The swallows were devoted parents, attentive to every squawk and squeal of a baby bird. Pairs shared responsibilities, one sitting on the nest while the other foraged.

The energy of the swallows amazed me. They seemed always to be in motion. Even while sitting on their nests their bodies quivered and their round, dark eyes blinked repeatedly, as if the birds were prepared at any moment to fly into the air.

My Mud Oven

My father was an architect, along with being a rancher and a pig farmer. He liked to build things. He never tired of putting up new structures on our place, and most of them were made of adobe bricks.

In his philosophy, children needed to be taught useful things, like how to dig a straight ditch and how to make an adobe wall stay upright. He gave us jobs to do, chores that stayed the same from one year to the next. Once in a while he gave us another sort of task, one that involved construction.

When I was ten I was given the job of building a mud oven. The Spanish word for this kind of oven is *horno.* It's a short, igloolike structure with a smoke hole in the top and a small, rounded opening on the side that serves as a door. *Hornos* are made with mud bricks (adobes) and then plastered on the outside with mud, so they end up looking like smooth-textured beehives.

I took on the job with deep misgivings. I knew better than to complain, because I knew he wouldn't stand for it. If I was at a loss as to how to build a *horno,* it was my responsibility to figure it out.

I went around our neighborhood looking at *hornos.* Most people who had them used them for firing clay objects as well as for baking fat round loaves of bread. They tended to be built at the corners of houses, so they blended in and did not seem like an addition.

I realized, after my survey of the neighborhood, that my first problem was to figure out where my *horno* ought to go.

Bill, the wrangler, helped me. He saw me with a bewildered look on my face, wandering around from one section of the ranch to another, and he suggested a solution when I told him my trouble:

"Put it by the side of the kitchen where it might turn out useful. And besides, you'll have the kitchen wall to help hold it up."

I thought this was brilliant.

We had an adobe-making "factory" on our place. Most people in those days made their own adobe bricks. You mix "clean" dirt with sand, with more dirt than sand. You add a little bit of straw and some water. The mixing of the mud is fun because adobe mud smells delicious and feels good to the touch.

You work the mud, pulling all the ingredients together in a

wooden trough on the ground. The trough is long and low and has a sheet of tin nailed to the floor. You use a special hoe with two holes in it, so the soft, brown mud goes squashing through the holes as well as being pushed and pulled.

I loved the mixing part.

Pouring the mud into forms was heavy work. I almost needed help to get it done. I shoveled the mud into a wheelbarrow with steep sides and then slopped it into wooden frames that lay flat on the ground.

The sun was hot on my back while I toiled away, making sure each square in the frames was well loaded with mud. The workmen in the adobe yard gave me encouragement. Sometimes they leaned on the handles of their hoes to watch me, tolerant smiles on their faces.

It took many days for the adobe bricks to dry and season inside the forms. When they're ready you have to pull off the forms, which

Adobe wall

Adobe oven, Taos Pueblo, New Mexico.

is almost as hard as pouring. Adobes break, and you save these fragments to throw into the next trough of mud.

Finally I had about fifty perfectly shaped adobe bricks for my *horno.* Each weighed about twenty pounds. I used the wheelbarrow to transport the adobes to the building site.

I set a ring of adobes on the ground to form a half circle and mixed mud to use as mortar. I spread this on the surface of the adobes so the next layer would bond with the first. Mortar is the same mud mixture the adobes are made with, only with more water added.

I was glad for the kitchen wall, which formed an already complete side of the *horno* and gave it support to lean against.

I forgot the door opening and made the base too big. Then I made it too small. It took two false starts to get the walls rising.

Everything went well until I came to the shaping of the dome roof. The concept of building an igloo was beyond me. I remembered pictures of famous dome roofs in books and wondered how they'd been built so perfectly.

Everything I tried failed. I ended up sitting on the ground, next to my partly done *horno,* with tears running down my face. Once again Bill saved me.

Bill stood in the blazing sun scratching his chin and squinting in a way I recognized. It was the look he got when he was solving a problem. Finally he said, "I think I know what you need to do."

At his direction I broke whole adobes into halves and quarters, losing some because I shattered them to bits. Bill let me use his hatchet and his knife. I was able to fit the adobe pieces together like parts to a puzzle, with mortar between for glue. We got sticks to keep the roof propped and in position until it dried.

The plastering was the best part, sheer joy compared to

struggling with the dome. The plaster mud went on like lotion onto rough skin.

When I was ready I told my father to come and see the completed *horno.* I confessed that Bill had helped me.

"That's okay," he said. "You've learned something useful: how to build your own mud house."

"My own house? You mean I could put my own entire house together if I wanted?" I replied, unaware that building the horno had taught me so much.

"You could start today, from what you've learned."

I felt proud over my success, and immediately built a fire inside the *horno* to make sure it really worked. It did. The smoke went out the smoke hole exactly as it was supposed to.

I go back to see the *horno* I built when I was young. Other people own the ranch now. New kids are growing up where I did. The oven looks a little the worse for all the seasons of rain that have washed down its mud sides, and there's a broad swatch of soot over the front door. The soot tells me the oven is still used, after all this time.

4. Magic Mud

Tracks

I crept along barefoot on the mud. It was a summer night with no moon. I followed my friend Miguel along the edge of the Rio Grande. I held a broomstick in one hand, tight in my fingers. It was rigged as a spear. Miguel had one too. He'd made them. They were wooden handles with knives tied to one end.

"Let's go get frogs," Miguel had said at dusk.

"Sure," I agreed, not knowing his intention was to slaughter them. When he stuck the spear in my hand, I figured out what he meant to do, but Miguel had me mesmerized that summer. I couldn't say no. It was that simple.

"We'll skin 'em and eat 'em," he promised.

I shuddered, but I kept quiet, nodding like a person with no opinions of her own.

We crossed sloppy, loose mud that worked itself between my toes like plaster. I sank to my ankles, and when I pulled a foot out, gurgling noises filled the darkness around us. The sounds were such that only a deaf frog would miss them.

I heard the plopping of frogs escaping into the river's wide stream. Smart frogs, I thought, making clean getaways.

(above) Mountain lion tracks, Paradise Flats, Capitol Reef National Park, Utah. (below) Raven and small mammal tracks, Cottonwood Wash, Capitol Reef National Park, Utah.

No dumb frogs were out that night.

We gave up hunting and turned on our flashlights so we could explore the mud for tracks. This was a favorite pastime of mine. The riverside mud was crisscrossed with all sorts of animal tracks, signs of creatures moving about, frogs, insects, birds, raccoons, skunks, and coyotes. You could read the mud like a page in a book, pick up a trail, follow it, and figure out what animal made it.

The mud was a regular expressway of tracks. Their nature changed all the time. Trying to decide the meanings of the marks on the mud was a game to me, and a lot more fun than trying to stab frogs in the back.

Miguel explained that where he came from, which was Florida, people ate frogs almost daily. "My mother has lots of ways to fix frogs for eating," he told me. "She likes it when I bring some home."

I forgave him. It turned out it wasn't his fault he went looking for frogs to kill. It was cultural, like my family's eating pork chops or bacon. Soon Miguel's mind was off frogs. He was as interested in track reading as I was.

"Look," I said, pointing and stepping forward carefully so I didn't smear away the tracks. "Some animal, a shrew or a mouse, got captured from above. See? The tracks run along and then stop, poof, just like that, and there aren't any others!"

We had such a good time, we went back at sunset the next day to hide in the willows and see if we could see animals in action. We concealed ourselves and stayed still so even the shyest animals wouldn't know we were there.

A two-foot-tall heron dressed in white, green, and black feathers stepped from the shadows of the reeds by the water. It walked with a jerky motion, its beady eyes unblinking.

The heron stopped and stood motionless where the water

lapped the muddy bank. Suddenly it struck at the water with its slender bill and caught a tiny fish. The bird took two more fish from the river before it turned and slipped back into the reeds, its long toes leaving distinct marks in the mud.

We saw a mother skunk with three babies stepping along behind her. The babies held their tails high just the way their mother did, as if they were displaying furry flags.

My heart nearly stopped beating when a pair of coyotes came out of the scrubby brush above the riverbank and stepped down to the water to drink.

It was not quite full dark when we saw a bullsnake capture a toad. The toad hopped from a hiding place and sat on the mud, resting and looking around. In a flash too swift to see, the bullsnake slithered across the mud and took the toad into its jaws. The snake took its time swallowing the toad, its mouth stretched beyond belief.

The mud mirrored the lives of animals, from the four-legged kind to great horned owls on silent wings snatching mice into their talons from the air. Trying to understand what stories the marks on the mud told made me feel closer to those "others" with which we share the planet.

white-throated woodrat tracks

Striped skunk tracks

Mud Games

My twin sisters and I were strongly attached to the physical world of our childhood, to the way it smelled, tasted, sounded, and looked. Natalie and Kim loved the stink of the lower pasture, the feel of horsehide, and saddle leather under their fingers as much as I did. It felt good to scratch newborn piglets behind the ears, where the skin was especially soft. The smell of fresh-cut hay was heady and fine. Winter fires burning pinon pine filled the air with sweet scents as familiar as the sunrise.

Mud was something we more than loved. It was the essential element of many of our games and pastimes. We lived in mud houses, leaned against mud walls, walked through mud most times of the year, and knew it as we knew the air, free and all around us.

No mud was rejected. Even the blackest, foulest mud, with animal droppings mixed into it, had a certain character we liked.

Mud was a refuge. When my sisters argued with me and my feelings got hurt, I went to the irrigation ditch to slip in and sit, up to the knees in slime, my fingers pressed into the giving warmth of the muddy banks. This always made me feel better.

Mud was a disguise. It was a way to alter one's appearance by smearing it from head to toe. We painted our arms, legs, faces, backs, and fronts with fantastic designs. We mixed food coloring with mud to make weird hues, a ritual that had a mystical meaning impossible to put into words.

And then there were the mud wars.

The mud wars began with a neighborhood crisis. New kids moved into the area, and they were brats. They slipped through the fences and chased our cows. They hid behind trees to ambush us when we went horseback riding.

Six-year-old girl
making mud hand
prints, Oljeto Wash,
San Juan River,
Navajo Indian
Reservation, Utah.

Eight-year-old girl
making mud balls,
LaVerkin Falls,
Greater Zion
Wilderness, Utah.

My sister Natalie said, "Let's build a mud fort in the pasture and challenge those kids to a war." We nodded in agreement. "We can make mud balls for throwing," she added, grinning evilly.

We built a fort with little trouble, using plywood propped up on sections of two-by-fours with river stones to secure it. The mud balls proved more difficult.

Days passed before we figured out the best mud-ball recipe. The soft earth had to be mixed with just the right amount of sand and water or the balls would not dry properly or stay firm and together.

Here is our recipe for the perfect mud ball:

Three pails of soil from the hills across the road.

One pail of sand from the riverbed.

Half a pail of water from the irrigation ditch. (Plain water from a hose has no silt in it, so it does not work as well.)

Mix all ingredients together with your hands, and keep on mixing until you get tired. Let the mud rest for ten or fifteen minutes and then mix some more. Roll the mud in the palms of your hands without poking it with your fingers and shape it into spheres the size of golf balls. Set these in rows in a shady place where they can dry slowly. (If they dry too fast they crack.) The best place for drying is a milk room or a laundry room, where the atmosphere is humid.

With a stack of mud balls piled behind us in the plywood fort, we were ready to face the new kids in the neighborhood. They were eager to engage us.

There were no serious injuries, only a lot of mud balls flying back and forth. We stopped for meals, to relieve ourselves, and to sleep in our own beds at night; otherwise we went at it, flinging small brown missiles at each other for four days running.

On the fifth day, with the sun low in the sky, each of us

apparently had the feeling that we were getting nowhere with our war. One of the enemy came away from the barrier their group had raised. He picked up globs of wet mud and tossed them into the air. In that moment everybody forgot the original protest. We all ran out to indulge in a freethrow of mud.

There was an outburst of elation, of spontaneous joy. It was exuberance without malice, only fun. The war ended and peace was declared.

Before long the new kids were considered old-timers. Friendships grew and rancor died.

The new kids joined in the mud games we'd invented, sharing our passion for seeing how far we could sink into a mud hole without disappearing or playing gushy women.

This last was one of the more disgusting games we'd dreamed up. It involved pretending we were cows making cow pies, which some call meadow muffins. We found a particular kind of mud, with the appropriate texture and weight, and held it in the air above our shoulders. We let it plop to the earth from this height. The sound it made pleased us.

It's hard to explain why we called this game Gushy Women. Maybe it was because my sisters and I, the inventors of it, were girls. In addition, girls favored playing the game ten to one over boys.

My sisters and I used our tracking skills to play a game we called Cowboys and Indians. One of us went off alone to become "lost," and the others set out to find her. This was a game that could last a full summer day. One rule was to leave footprints in mud, so there would always be a trace of where you were headed, clues for those who followed.

My mother is now over ninety years old. She recently told me a story about my father's affection for mud, a thing I wasn't aware of

Kids playing in pothole, Toroweap Point, Grand Canyon National Park, Arizona.

when I was little. He so loved playing in muck and mire that my mother nicknamed him "He Who Sinks Out of Sight in Mud."

Medicine Mud

"It's magic," Natalie said, her eyes wide with wonder. She let the slick red mud slip through her fingers and slide down her arms. "I know it is, just feel it." She touched a bit of the mud to her tongue with a fingertip. "It even tastes like medicine mud."

"It's the mud that heals wounds, for sure," Kim agreed.

"Prove it," I challenged. "How can you be so positive unless you see it working?"

"Mom and Dad said this mud heals wounds. You heard them," Natalie answered.

She was telling the truth, but I wanted to see the power of the mud with my own eyes.

We were on a two-week family camping trip in southern Utah. I was eight, and Kim and Natalie were ten. We'd driven for two days on twisty roads through the slickrock canyons and towering mesas of southern Utah. On the way, our parents spoke of the medicine mud, saying it was used to treat all sorts of physical troubles. The mud could be found only in Utah. Nobody understood how it worked: the power of medicine mud was a mystery.

Their conversation caught our interest. Parents hardly ever spoke respectfully of mud. They described what the medicine mud looked like and said people came from all over the world to take it away. We listened and wondered if we might find this magical mud ourselves.

At the end of the third day we camped on a platform of rock at the edge of a deep canyon. The next morning our parents shooed us off, saying, "Go and explore. Find something to do by yourselves for a few hours." They did not appear concerned that we might become lost. I think they were too eager to be rid of us after the hours of confinement in the car.

We loaded our knapsacks with canteens and left camp determined to search for the mysterious medicine mud.

We set off single file, Natalie in the lead. We walked under a blazing hot sun through narrow, winding canyons and across grassy flats ringed by sandstone formations.

Natalie spotted it first. We were scrambling up a smooth boulder the size of a small car, using cracks to squeeze bare toes into and bumps and ridges to grasp with our fingers. My sister's voice rang out, echoing off the cliffs around us. "There it is!" she screamed.

The mud lay pooled in shallow basins on the top of the boulder. It was the same pale strawberry-red color we'd heard described. It shimmered in the light. The texture was silky smooth and lovely, like a rich red pudding.

"I want to see it work," I insisted.

"Who has a cut or a rash?" Natalie asked, her hands and arms heavily drenched in medicine mud. She checked her own body for these infirmities.

We examined one another. The examinations were simple because we each wore cotton shorts and nothing else. Our feet were bare.

"Nobody has anything wrong," Kim said. "Maybe we can save some mud. We can fill our canteens and take it back to camp with us. Later we can find ways to see it work."

That plan was approved.

We stepped into the mud-filled basins in the rocks and flattened ourselves against the warmth of the sandstone to let the mud wash over us. I imagined it felt the same as being dipped in a vat of expensive skin cream.

The mud was more liquid than solid. It slipped into our wide-necked canteens like fresh oil, making a gurgling sound as it went in, a murmur that helped convince us of its importance.

We started back toward camp at about three in the afternoon (going by the position of the sun) and knew almost immediately that we were lost.

"It's that way," Kim said.

"No, it's that way, I know it is," Natalie insisted.

"You're both wrong," I chimed in. "I kept track. Remember that tree over there, the big one? And the rock wall over there? The one with those deep cracks in it? We passed by those rocks when we came from over that way."

We settled the discussion by climbing to the top of a "lookout" rock and peering into the distance in every direction. We selected what seemed the right way to go and started off.

We made it into camp just as the sun was setting. Our parents were beside themselves with worry.

"We were sure you three were lost," my father said, giving us a long, hard look. "Were you? Or did you just lose track of the time?"

My mouth was beginning to form a response when Natalie burst out, "We were lost for a while, meaning we didn't know which way to go, but the medicine mud saved us."

Kim and I looked at Natalie with unbelieving eyes.

"The what?" both parents said at once.

"The medicine mud. We went to find it, and we did find it. Remember, you told us about the mud in the car? We decided to bring some back, since we don't have any cuts or wounds. I'm positive we were saved by having the mud with us. If we hadn't brought some back, we'd be out there still. We'd be lost, for sure."

My sister sounded utterly convinced of what she was saying. I fell under the spell of her words.

"She's delirious," my mother said.

"A crazy story if you ask me," my father said.

"It's the mud that did it," I said seriously.

"Let's have a look at this mud," my father said.

We showed him what we had in our canteens. We let some drip on his hands. He smelled the mud. He tasted it. He did not punish us for causing worry. I wondered if he believed it, about the mud helping us find camp. I myself believed it. I was convinced.

We camped four days on the platform of rock, taking day hikes into the wilderness. My sisters and I searched and found more medicine mud.

We filled every available container we could wrangle away from camp. Natalie said, "I have a plan." She wouldn't tell us what it was until our last day in Utah.

"We're going to bottle it," she said. "We'll sell it. People will buy the mud because we'll say how it works for every human ailment, even warts." Natalie had recently had a wart burned off her hand, which is probably why she mentioned warts in particular. "You heard what Dad said. People come from other countries to get this mud. It's powerful and old. People will pay a lot for it because it's magic and mysterious. We'll make so much money, we won't have to work for the rest of our lives."

Kim grinned, the expectation of great wealth glowing in her eyes.

"We have to bottle it and put labels on the bottles. What should we name it?" Kim asked.

"It already has a name," I interjected, eager for a small part in

Sunlight filtering into badlands slot, Cathedral Gorge State Park, Nevada.

the scheme to be rich. "It's officially Medicine Mud."

"Sounds good to me," Natalie said, hefting a plastic water jug of the stuff into the back of the car.

In the storage room off the kitchen, we helped ourselves to as many canning jars as we needed to set up our secret business selling bottled Medicine Mud.

One neighbor bought some to make her freckles go away. Another person wanted some for arthritis. We sold it to relieve sunburn and diaper rash, as a cure for pink eye, to rid dogs of fleas and children of lice, and to soothe saddle sores on horses. I don't remember hearing about any miracle cures brought on by the mud, but we remained sure there wasn't anything it couldn't fix—until our father discovered what we were up to.

He confronted us, waving a jar of the mud in front of our faces. He yelled at us and demanded to know how we could engage in a "moral deception" and "bilk" poor people out of their hard-earned cash, lying about the virtues of plain old Utah slickrock canyon mud.

"It's Medicine Mud," I said, bewildered by his anger. "You said so yourself. The mud helped us get out of the wilderness that time, remember?"

He looked at me in silence, as if my eight-and-a-half-year-old mind had slipped a hinge. He looked at the three of us, considering what punishment would fit the crime.

The twins refused to speak, so I continued with my defense of our behavior. "The mud is old, you said so," I insisted, tears starting. "It was used by prehistoric people. There isn't any mud like this in New Mexico. I don't see what's so bad about selling it if it helps people. It does help people. You and Mom said it does."

He relented. He smiled at us. I detected a trace of pride in his eyes. "The Three Entrepreneurs," he said quietly. He left us standing there shivering with relief. His scoldings could be harsh. We got off easy. His last word was, "No more selling this stuff for money, understand? You can give it away, but you cannot sell it."

He took a jar of our mud with him. He kept it. When I was no longer afraid of reviving his anger about our Medicine Mud business, I asked him what *entrepreneurs* means.

"It means enterprising, thinking up new ideas, new schemes. It means being good business people."

It was my turn to be proud.

His discovery ended our business, but we had mud left over. We used it to initiate two girl cousins from the East Coast who came to visit us. They were pale skinned, blue eyed, and afraid of spiders. They wouldn't dare play kick the can after the sun went down. To them everything was scary and dangerous.

The initiation was painless. Smooth, slick, red Utah mud was emptied out of a jar, applied to the top of the head, and allowed to drip slowly down over the face, neck, and shoulders. The initiate was not permitted to move, except to breathe and blink. We told our cousins the mud was magic, that it would coat them with courage.

We said they would never feel fear again, adding that the power of the mud might wear off, but they were welcome to come back the next summer and get another treatment.

In our childhood being brave meant doing things like holding a tarantula in the palm of your hand without screaming or jerking around, or dropping into a mud hole and showing no panic if you sank to your neck. Judging by our standards, which were high, the mud-soaking ritual was a success. Once drenched with Medicine Mud, the cousins were as brave as any kids we knew.

A Glossary of
Mud Words

mud—A slimy, sticky, fluid to plastic substance that is a mixture of finely divided particles of solid materials and water. A wet, soft, earthly matter; mire; dregs; marsh; semifluid; dirt; ooze; slime; sludge; slush.

baseball mud—Mud taken from a particular stretch of the Delaware River and used to coat and "season" new baseballs before the game. All baseball teams in the major leagues use Delaware River mud this way.

mud bath—A medicinal bath of heated mud.

mud crawlers—Military men marching in wet weather; earthworms.

mudder—A racehorse that runs well in mud or on a muddy track.

muddle—A confusing situation. To muddle on is to keep going and not give up.

muddlehead—A stupid person.

muddler—A clumsy, awkward person.

mud dredger—A machine for dredging mud.

muddy—Dull spirited and easily confused.

Creek-bed near Sandy Ranch, Capitol Reef National Park, Utah.

mud fever—A condition of having raw, red skin after spending too much time in mud.

mud flap—A sheet of thin material suspended behind the rear wheels of vehicles, usually trucks, intended to catch spatters of mud.

mud gunner—A machine gunner.

Mudhead—One of a Zuni or Hopi clown clan who appears daubed in mud and represents a rain priest, a messenger from the Underworld, or human characteristics in reverse.

mud hole—A saltwater lagoon where whales were once captured. A wallow or puddle of muddy water where animals go to cool off on hot, dry days.

mud honey—Slush following a thaw.

mud hook—A boat anchor.

mud hop—A worker who keeps track of arriving and departing trains

mud island—A nickname for London's South End, the poorest district in the city.

mud lark—A waterfront thief; one who hides under ships to buy stolen goods from sailors; a person who scavenges in the gutter; a cleaner of sewers; a fool; a child of poor parents.

mud lava—Mud that is ejected from a volcano.

mud opera or *mud show*—An old-time circus, a traveling show.

mud pads—The feet of the lower classes (British).

mud pipes—The boots of the lower classes (British).

mud plunging—Tramping through the mud in search of handouts.

mudroom—A small room attached to a house, used for the storage of boots, rain gear, and other outdoor clothing likely to be smeared with mud.

mudsill—The lowest timber or sill on the foundation of a structure.

mudslinger—A person who uses unflattering remarks about others.

mudstone—A geological term for a hardened sedimentary rock formed from clay and similar to shale.

mud student—Someone, male or female, who is studying to become a farmer.

Plants and Animals Named After Mud

These organisms are commonly found in muddy places.

mud buttercup (Ranunculus sceleratus)—A one to three-inch-tall swamp or marsh buttercup with weak stems and glossy, yellow flowers pollinated by bees or wasps.

mud cat (Notorus stigmosus)—A catfish that favors muddy water.

mud coot (Gallinula chloropus)—A yellow-legged, dull-colored waterbird that lives in freshwater marshes, ponds, and rivers; common in brackish (part salt) water.

mud crab (Eurypanopeus depressus)—A kind of freshwater crab that burrows into the mud.

mud dauber (Sceliphron caementarium)—A kind of wasp that uses mud mixed with saliva to build a nest for its eggs and young; any of several species of wasp with four wings, two antennae, two forelegs, and four additional legs, threadwaisted, black-and-blue satin color; not harmful.

mud fish—Any of a number of freshwater fish, such as *Hypomesus olidus,* that swims and lingers near the bottom of muddy rivers.

mud frog (Pelobated fuscus)—A European frog that favors mud.

mud hen—Birds that live in marshes, such as coots, rails, marsh hens, and gallinules *(Porphyrula martinica)*; also, a female speculator on the stock market.

mud horsetail (Equisetum fluviatile)—Plants with hollow-jointed stems and whorls of slender branches at the joints, resembling a horse's tail.

mud iguana or *mud siren (Siren Lacertina)*—A Southern states salamander that lives in ponds, rivers, and swamps; this salamander has only front legs, no back legs.

mud puppy (Necturus)—A salamander that lives in North America; it is large (3-4 inches long) and has black skin with bright yellow spots.

mud sedge (Cyperaceae)—Various coarse, grassy, rushlike or flaglike plants growing in wet places.

mudskipper (Periophthalmus and Boleophthalmus)—A fish that lives on the shores of Malaysian seas; it skips on the mud when the tide is out, using a muscular tail and front fins shaped like legs.

mud snake (Farancia abacura)—A burrowing swamp snake that feeds on frogs and fish.

mud sucker—Any bird living an aquatic life that finds it food in mud.

mud swallow (Hirundo pyrrhonota)—A cliff swallow that uses mud mixed with saliva to make nests on cliff walls.

mud turtle (Kinosternon subrubrum)—Any of a variety of freshwater turtles that like to burrow and settle in mud when resting or hiding.

mudwort (Limosella aguntica)—A plant found growing in muddy environments.

Index